QUIZPEDIA

AISLING COUGHLAN

THE
00s

THE ULTIMATE
BOOK OF TRIVIA

T0002637

Smith
Street
Books

SO YOU THINK YOU KNOW ...

WORLD EVENTS

Quiz 01

1.
In what year did the Euro first circulate as physical currency?

2.
A hot topic in 2007/2008, what does GFC stand for?

3.
How many planes were hijacked on September 11 2001?

4.
What change happened to Pluto in 2006?

5.
Which country became the first to fully legalize same-sex marriage in 2001?

6.
Who succeeded Pope John Paul II after his death in 2005?

7.
On what date did the London bombings take place?

8.
What type of aircraft ceased operating in October 2003?

9.
The Indian Ocean tsunami occurred on what date of 2004?

10.
The 2004 Athens Olympics marked what anniversary of the games?

SO YOU THINK
YOU KNOW ...

ACTION
MOVIES

"*I WILL HAVE MY VENGEANCE, IN THIS LIFE OR THE NEXT*"

Quiz 02

1.
"I will look for you, I will find you, and I will kill you" are lines from which 2008 movie?

2.
Angelina Jolie played which video game character in the live-action movie version?

3.
Aside from *Casino Royale*, what two other Bond movies were released in the 2000s?

4.
Who directed *Snatch* and *RocknRolla*?

5.
Kathryn Bigelow won the Best Director Oscar for which 2008 movie?

6.
Dominic "Dom" Toretto and Brian O'Conner were lead characters in which 2001 movie which has (so far) sparked nine follow-ups?

7.
Halle Berry donned the mask of which well-known character in 2004?

8.
Matt Damon made his debut in 2002 as which fictional character created by Robert Ludlum?

9.
What is the name given to the psychics who see the future in *Minority Report*?

10.
Who played the bad guy to Russell Crowe's good guy in *Gladiator*?

SO YOU THINK
YOU KNOW ...

BOOKS
FOR KIDS

Quiz 03

1.
What are the names of the other two books in the Mockingjay trilogy after *The Hunger Games*?

2.
What year was the last Harry Potter book published?

3.
Which 2001 book was described by its Irish author as *Die Hard* with fairies?

4.
A man who brings book characters to life just by reading them aloud is the plot of which 2003 book, later a movie starring Brendan Fraser?

5.
According to author Mo Willems, who should you not let drive the bus?

6.
2003's *Lyra's Oxford* is the follow-up to which best-selling trilogy by Philip Pullman?

7.
Which book was the first in the series published in 2007 by author and cartoonist Jeff Kinney?

8.
Who illustrated *The Boy in the Dress*, the first children's book written by David Walliams?

9.
Whose offspring got their own Julia Donaldson picture book in 2004?

10.
Forks, Washington, is the often-overcast setting for which trio of books?

SO YOU THINK YOU KNOW ...

HIGH SCHOOL DRAMA

Quiz 04

1.
The Dillon Panthers and their coach, Coach Taylor, are the protagonists of which high school drama?

2.
Amy Sherman-Palladino created which fast-talking, women-led long-running TV show?

3.
In *The OC*, what part of California does Ryan come from before moving to the wealthy Orange County (OC)?

4.
How many seasons did *The Inbetweeners* run for?

5.
Where was *Skins* set?

6.
Which coming of age show about the inhabitants of Capeside came to an end in 2003?

7.
Who narrated *Gossip Girl*?

8.
Which classic 1990s show with a famous postcode got a re-boot in 2008?

9.
A high school student moonlights as a private eye in which show?

10.
Half-brothers Nathan and Lucas share a love of basketball in which TV show set in a small town?

SO YOU THINK
YOU KNOW ...

ACADEMY
AWARDS

Quiz 05

1.
In 2003, what musical became the first movie since 1968's *Oliver* to win Best Picture?

2.
Why did 2001 Best Original Song nominee Björk make headlines on the red carpet?

3.
Russell Crowe won the 2001 Best Actor award for his portrayal of which character?

4.
True or false: *Brokeback Mountain* won Best Picture in 2006?

5.
Nicole Kidman won the Best Actress Oscar in 2003 for portraying which literary figure?

6.
In 2007 Martin Scorsese had his only Best Director win to date, for which movie?

7.
Halle Berry won Best Actress for which 2001 movie?

8.
2008's Best Picture *Slumdog Millionaire* is set around which TV game show format?

9.
Who was posthumously awarded the Best Supporting Actor Oscar in 2009?

10.
The Best Makeup award in 2009 went to which movie, starring Brad Pitt and Cate Blanchett?

SO YOU THINK
YOU KNOW ...

COMEDY
MOVIES

"THEY'VE DONE STUDIES, YOU KNOW. 60 PERCENT OF THE TIME, IT WORKS EVERY TIME."

Quiz 06

1.
Who has many leather-bound books and an apartment that smells of rich mahogany?

2.
Armed and Fabulous is the tagline for the 2005 sequel to which 2000 movie?

3.
What country does fictional journalist Borat come from?

4.
Jennifer Coolidge plays manicurist Paulette Bonafonté in which 2001 movie?

5.
What's Derek Zoolander's trademark look?

6.
A family road trip in a yellow Volkswagen to attend a beauty pageant is the plot of which 2006 movie?

7.
A movie of what long-running animated show created in 1987 was released in 2007?

8.
The Life Aquatic with Steve Zissou features a hunt for what animal?

9.
Which two actors swap places in 2003's *Freaky Friday*?

10.
Boris the Blade, Brick Top Pulford and Franky Four-Fingers are characters in which 2000 movie?

SO YOU THINK YOU KNOW ...

MEN'S FASHION

Quiz 07

1.
Which teen singing sensation inspired a million side-swept haircuts?

2.
What kind of 1970s hat, often fabric in the front and mesh in the back, became popular in the early 2000s?

3.
Which popular brand featured vintage tattoo-style designs?

4.
What color were the swimming trunks worn by Daniel Craig as Agent 007 as he emerged from the ocean in *Casino Royale*?

5.
The checked pattern of which British fashion label became one of the most counterfeited?

6.
What portmanteau to describe a well-groomed man became popular after it was used to describe David Beckham in 2002?

7.
Which heavyweight boxer got a tribal tattoo on his face in 2003?

8.
Which comedian made headlines sporting a lime green mankini?

9.
What did *South Park* co-creator Trey Parker wear to the Academy Awards in 2000?

10.
Sean John was the in-demand menswear label from which rap star?

SO YOU THINK
YOU KNOW ...

SPORTS

Quiz 08

1.
How many of Lance Armstrong's seven Tour de France wins took place in the 2000s?

2.
Who lit the Olympic cauldron at the opening of the 2000 Games in Sydney?

3.
In 2009, "Bloodgate", where a player used fake blood to fake an injury, occurred in which sport?

4.
Which professional golfer became the youngest player to win all four majors championships?

5.
Which British distance runner, awarded an MBE in 2002, retired in 2005?

6.
Michael Jordan ended his career with which basketball team in 2003?

7.
How many times in the 2000s did a Williams sister win the Wimbledon singles trophy?

8.
Which sprinter's trademark pose made its first appearance at the 2008 Beijing Olympics?

9.
In what year did Stephanie Gilmore win her first World Surfing League championship?

10.
Which record-breaking athlete has the nickname The Baltimore Bullet?

REALITY TV GAMES

"I WAS ROOTING FOR YOU, WE WERE ALL ROOTING FOR YOU!"

Quiz 09

1.
Nea Marshall Kudi Ngwa, better known as BeBe Zahara Benet, was the winner of the inaugural season of which competition?

2.
Which competitive show ended with a contestant being told: "You're fired"?

3.
Susan Boyle rose to fame after appearing on what show?

4.
Where was the first season of *Survivor* filmed?

5.
The host of which TV show is credited with coining the term "smize" meaning to smile with your eyes?

6.
On *The Biggest Loser*, you win if you lose the most what?

7.
Simon Cowell, Louis Walsh and Sharon Osbourne were the judges of which talent show?

8.
What was the prize for the winners of *The Amazing Race*?

9.
British DJ Tony Blackburn beat his fellow celebrity rivals, including Uri Geller and Nigel Benn, to win what survival show?

10.
On what dating show were the contestants competing for the affection of a fake millionaire?

SO YOU THINK
YOU KNOW ...

HIP-HOP
AND RAP

Quiz 10

1.
Who wanted to see you "In Da Club"?

2.
Eminem's "Stan" sampled which song by which British singer?

3.
Which artist is part of both The Neptunes and N.E.R.D.?

4.
Whose stage name is a portmanteau of chameleon and millionaire?

5.
Ms Jackson, the subject of the 2000 Outkast song, is reportedly an apology to the mother of which American singer songwriter?

6.
The music video for which Wu-Tang Clan song saw them hanging out in a stone age–like environment?

7.
Who sang the 2001 hit "Get Ur Freak On"?

8.
By what stage name does Scott Ramon Seguro Mescudi go by?

9.
Snoop Dogg sang about dropping it like it was hot. What was he talking about?

10.
Eve and Alicia Keys teamed up for which 2002 song?

SO YOU THINK
YOU KNOW ...

THE NEW AGE OF SOCIAL MEDIA

Quiz 11

1.
Which university was Mark Zuckerberg attending when he created Facebook?

2.
What was Bebo a backronym for?

3.
How many characters were initially allowed on Twitter posts when it launched in 2006?

4.
Who was everybody's first friend when they joined Myspace?

5.
Which football player featured in the Nike ad that was the most watched YouTube video in the year of its launch in 2005?

6.
Which website, launched in 2003, became the social network for getting a job?

7.
What did people start uploading onto Flickr in 2003?

8.
In what year was Facebook made available to the public?

9.
Which micro-blogging site was launched by 21-year-old David Karp in 2007?

10.
Which matchmaking site first made an appearance in 2004?

SO YOU THINK
YOU KNOW ...

ROCK

Quiz 12

1.
What fictitious metal did 3 Doors Down sing about in 2000?

2.
Name the female vocalist from Evanescence?

3.
Hybrid Theory was the debut album from which band in 2000?

4.
Which British town are the Arctic Monkeys from?

5.
What are the names of the twin brothers from Good Charlotte?

6.
Which band's 2004 rock opera album is about protagonist Jesus of Suburbia?

7.
Karen O is the lead singer of which band?

8.
The Foo Fighters' Dave Grohl is an alum of which 90s grunge band?

9.
Brandon Flowers fronts which band?

10.
Animated band Gorillaz was created by which artist?

TEEN

MOVIES

"MY EXPECTATION IN
LIFE IS TO BE INVISIBLE
... I'M GOOD AT IT"

Quiz 13

1.
What name is on the fake ID Fogell uses to buy alcohol in *Superbad*?

2.
In the *Twilight* world, how do you spot a vampire in daylight?

3.
Kirsten Dunst shows us the competitive world of what sport in *Bring It On*?

4.
Julie Andrews plays the Queen regent of fictional Genovia in which 2001 movie?

5.
What 2000 film is the setting in the music video for the Wheatus hit "Teenage Dirtbag"?

6.
In 2005's *Sisterhood of the Travelling Pants*, how many girls shared the pants?

7.
Who directed 2009's roller-derby flick *Whip It*?

8.
Mark Ruffalo's and Jennifer Garner's characters do what dance during *13 Going on 30*?

9.
A run-down amusement park in the summer of 1987 is the setting for which 2009 movie?

10.
Who plays Zac Efron's adult self in *17 Again*?

SO YOU THINK
YOU KNOW ...

WOMEN'S
FASHION

Quiz 14

1.
Who designed the famous green chiffon and silk dress, which closed only at the waist, worn by Jennifer Lopez to the Grammy Awards in 2000?

2.
The velour tracksuit favored by Paris Hilton and Kim Kardashian was a trademark of which brand?

3.
Which famous stylist got her own TV show in 2008?

4.
What does L.A.M.B., the fashion and accessory brand by Gwen Stefani, stand for?

5.
What is a Croydon Facelift?

6.
Samantha from *Sex and the City* abuses her relationship with client Lucy Liu to obtain what luxury fashion item?

7.
Which child of famous parents opened her fashion house in 2001, after a stint at Chloé?

8.
Sienna Miller became the pin-up for which trend?

9.
What was the trendy way to part your hair in the 2000s?

10.
Cowboy shirts, hats and rhinestone jeans were thrust into the 2000 spotlight by the release of which artist's album?

SO YOU THINK
YOU KNOW ...

AVATAR

Quiz 15

1.
In what year was
Avatar released?

2.
Who directed it?

3.
Adjusted for inflation,
Avatar is the second
highest grossing movie
of all time. What are
numbers 1 and 3?

4.
Visual effects were
provided by New Zealand
studio Weta. What other
blockbuster franchise did
they work on?

5.
Who plays central
protagonist Marine
Jake Sully?

6.
What is the name of the
planet it's set on?

7.
What is the name given to
the tribe that live there?

8.
What is the name of the
metal substance
the humans are trying
to mine?

9.
Why does Jake say yes
to the job of spying on
the Na'vi?

10.
Who composed the
soundtrack, having
previously worked with
the same director
on *Titanic*?

SO YOU THINK YOU KNOW ...

REALITY TV SOCIALITES

"WHERE'S THE BEACH?"

Quiz 16

1.
Name the two stars of
A Simple Life?

2.
Trista Sutter was the star
of the inaugural series
of which show, after
becoming a runner-up on
The Bachelor?

3.
Which show promised
to show you high school
life in the "real"
Orange County?

4.
Heidi Montag and
Spencer Pratt were
sometimes villains of
which show?

5.
In what year did
*Keeping Up With the
Kardashians* premiere?

6.
The Girls Next Door
featured the goings-on of
the women who lived in
which famous house?

7.
Snooki and JWoww
showed us around which
US region?

8.
What was the first of
several spin-offs featuring
various Kardashian family
members to be made?

9.
Newlyweds followed which
singing couple?

10.
Which daughter of British
rock royalty rose to fame
after the family opened
their doors to an MTV
camera crew in 2002?

SO YOU THINK
YOU KNOW ...

TOYS

Quiz 17

1.
Cloe, Yasmin, Jade and Sasha were the first four of which dolls who made their debut in 2001?

2.
What was the only way for cool kids to get around?

3.
What brightly colored rubber bands became an instant hit?

4.
Which company launched Bionicle, a range of humanoid action figures?

5.
Which boardgame based on a TV quiz show became an instant hit when it was launched in 2000?

6.
What was the name of the robotic dog, launched by Sega in 2005, that lit up and played music?

7.
Lego produced its first Harry Potter set in which year?

8.
Which TV twins had their own dolls in the early 2000s?

9.
What cards were the rival of Pokémon cards?

10.
Collecting cards that correspond with railway routes is the basic concept for which boardgame, launched in 2004?

SO YOU THINK YOU KNOW ...

POLITICS

Quiz 18

1.
In December 2000, which US state had its vote recount stopped, handing the presidency to George W Bush?

2.
Which prominent Pakistani politician was assassinated in December 2007?

3.
In 2000, who was the first directly elected Mayor of London?

4.
Angela Merkel was elected to what post in 2005, one she held until 2021?

5.
In 2008, which country's prime minister offered an apology to its indigenous peoples for its history of mistreatment?

6.
Which international model became the first lady of France in 2008?

7.
Angelina Jolie became a Goodwill Ambassador to which agency in 2001?

8.
What British overseas territory voted with a 98% majority to remain a part of Britain over joining its neighbor, Spain?

9.
In what year did Barack Obama assume office as the president of the United States?

10.
Who challenged and won a leadership election to go on to become the prime minister of the United Kingdom in 2007?

FANTASY MOVIES

"YOU'RE A WIZARD, HARRY"

Quiz 19

1.
How many movies from the Harry Potter franchise were released between 2000 and 2009?

2.
In the Pirates of the Caribbean franchise, what's unusual about Davy Jones's beard?

3.
In 2007, Ray Winstone played a computer-animated version of which hero of an Old English epic poem?

4.
Who plays the female lead in *Enchanted*?

5.
Ben Stiller takes up a night job where statues come to life in which 2006 movie?

6.
Kate Beckinsale stars as Selene, a vampire warrior, in which 2003 movie?

7.
Dwayne "The Rock" Johnson plays which character in a spin-off from *The Mummy* movie?

8.
The final instalment of the *Lord of the Ring* movies premiered in which city in December 2003?

9.
Dark fantasy movie *Pan's Labyrinth* is set in which country?

10.
What role does Tilda Swinton play in *The Chronicles of Narnia: The Lion, the Witch and the Wardrobe*?

TECHNOLOGY

Quiz 20

1.
In the 2000s, what would you most likely have been using site LimeWire for?

2.
What file-sharing application ceased trading in 2001 due to major copyright infringement issues?

3.
What did Jeff Bezos launch in November 2007?

4.
In what year was the iPod launched?

5.
What three gigabyte sizes did the first iPhone model come in?

6.
The HTC Dream was the first smartphone to have what?

7.
What overtook the DVD for at-home entertainment?

8.
What wearable fitness device was launched in 2009?

9.
In 2001, which company launched the Xbox?

10.
What knowledgeable website, still popular today, was launched on January 15 2001?

BOOKS
FOR ADULTS

Quiz 21

1.
Angels and Demons and *The Da Vinci Code* feature the adventures of which fictional character?

2.
Which Hilary Mantel book won the 2009 Booker Prize?

3.
What time-hopping novel written by David Mitchell was released in 2004?

4.
Name the first of Margaret Atwood's MaddAddam trilogy, published in 2003.

5.
Shadow Moon is the main character in which Neil Gaiman fantasy, published in 2001?

6.
Who wrote *White Teeth*?

7.
Which 2003 novel is told through the eyes of a 15-year-old boy with autism, who decides to investigate the death of a neighbor's dog?

8.
What three countries does the main character visit in *Eat, Pray, Love*?

9.
Which author's books, all published posthumously in 2003, were the start of the Millennium series?

10.
Director Peter Jackson adapted which 2002 novel into a movie starring Saoirse Ronan and Stanley Tucci?

SO YOU THINK
YOU KNOW ...

MEAN
GIRLS

"THAT'S SO FETCH"

Quiz 22

1.
Where has Cady been for the past 12 years before she returns to the US?

2.
Regina, Gretchen and Karen make up what social group at the high school?

3.
What song do Cady, Regina, Gretchen and Karen dance to at the Christmas concert?

4.
What kind of store does Janis work in at the mall?

5.
What 2002 book is the movie based on?

6.
Who wrote, and co-starred, in the movie?

7.
What does Cady convince Regina to eat, telling her it will help her lose weight?

8.
The contents of what item causes all hell to break loose at North Shore High?

9.
What crime is Ms Norbury investigated for?

10.
How does Regina get a spine injury?

TOM

HANKS

CLASSICS

Quiz 23

1.
Tom as FBI Agent Carl Hanratty chases criminal Frank Abagnale in which 2002 movie?

2.
Which duo directed Tom in 2004's black comedy crime movie *The Ladykillers*?

3.
Inspired by a true story, his character from *The Terminal* is stuck inside which US airport?

4.
In 2002 Tom won an Emmy Award for directing an episode of which limited TV series?

5.
True or false? Tom appeared as himself in 2007's *The Simpsons Movie*?

6.
Which older gent co-starred with Tom in *Road to Perdition*, which turned out to be the actor's last on-screen movie role?

7.
Which one-woman stand-up show did Tom develop into a box office hit, after being convinced to see it by his wife, Rita?

8.
Which two Dan Brown novels, starring Tom, were made into movies in the 2000s?

9.
What was the name of the ball in *Cast Away*?

10.
Who did Tom star opposite in *Charlie Wilson's War*?

SO YOU THINK
YOU KNOW ...

SCIENCE

AND

SPACE

Quiz 24

1.
What famous animal died
on February 14 2003?

2.
Entrepreneur Dennis Tito
became the first person in
2001 to pay to do what?

3.
What major international
scientific research
project was completed
in April 2003?

4.
How many people
perished aboard the
Space Shuttle Columbia
in 2003?

5.
To combat public smoking,
in 2004 what country
became the first in the
world to ban smoking in
enclosed workplaces?

6.
The Berlin patient
was a man who, it was
announced in 2008,
had been cured of what?

7.
The first of what kind of
transplant was successfully
performed in France
in 2005?

8.
The first instance of
what respiratory disease
was discovered in
November 2002?

9.
In what year was the first
HPV vaccine approved
for the public?

10.
In what year did the
exploration rovers Spirit
and Opportunity land
on Mars?

SO YOU THINK YOU KNOW ...

ANIMATED MOVIES

"THAT'LL DO DONKEY, THAT'LL DO"

Quiz 25

1.
Who was the original voice of Shrek, before his untimely death led to the casting of Mike Myers?

2.
Who voiced Lilo from *Lilo and Stitch*?

3.
A reoccurring joke through which animated movie franchise is a squirrel chasing an acorn?

4.
Billy Crystal and John Goodman voice best pals in which 2001 movie?

5.
Name the 2002 Oscar-winning movie that tells the story of a young girl's adventure into the world of Japanese folklore?

6.
Who voiced the rat in *Ratatouille*?

7.
Stop-motion film *Coraline* is based on a novella by which best-selling sci-fi author?

8.
Wes Anderson adapted which kids book for his first foray into animated movies?

9.
Marriage, child loss, depression and death are unlikely themes for the opening of which 2009 animated movie?

10.
Name the fish Ellen DeGeneres voiced from 2003's *Finding Nemo*.

SO YOU THINK
YOU KNOW ...

CELEB
COUPLES

Quiz 26

1.
Which uber-famous couple, both actors, tied the knot in Malibu in 2000?

2.
Lenny Kravitz dated which Aussie actress in the early noughties?

3.
Ben Affleck and Jennifer Lopez reportedly met on the set of which 2003 movie flop?

4.
Which two stars of *The Notebook* dated from 2005 to 2007?

5.
Where did Wills and Kate meet in 2001?

6.
Alanis Morrisette was engaged to which Canadian actor?

7.
Who did Britney Spears marry in 2004?

8.
Which Spice Girl dated Eddie Murphy?

9.
Who did Macaulay Culkin date for most of the 2000s?

10.
Brokeback Mountain brought together which two stars, who stayed together for three years and had a daughter?

SO YOU THINK
YOU KNOW ...

BIOPICS

Quiz 27

1.
The true tale of Christopher McCandless is told by which movie?

2.
Helen Mirren portrayed Queen Elizabeth II in *The Queen*, set amid which dramatic event?

3.
Who directed Sean Penn as Harvey Milk in 2008's *Milk*?

4.
Julie Taymor directed Salma Hayek as she portrayed which artist in a 2002 film?

5.
A French 2007 adaptation of which book of the same name tells the story of a man with locked-in syndrome?

6.
Which actor portrayed Tony Wilson in 2002's *24 Hour Party People*?

7.
Contaminated water in Hinkley, California is the catalyst for the plot of which 2000 biopic?

8.
Philip Seymour Hoffman won an Oscar for portraying Truman Capote, during Capote's writing of which book?

9.
Michael Fassbender played Northern Irish inmate Bobby Sands in which 2008 movie?

10.
Who portrayed Katharine Hepburn in 2004's *The Aviator*?

SO YOU THINK YOU KNOW ...

SMALL SCREEN DRAMA

"I AM THE ONE WHO KNOCKS"

Quiz 28

1.
Jimmy McNulty and Bunk Moreland are characters in which show set in Baltimore?

2.
Who plays Nancy, the central character in *Weeds*?

3.
What's serial killer Dexter's day job?

4.
What event sees a group of people living on a desert island in *Lost*?

5.
Jennifer Garner plays Sydney Bristow, a CIA double agent in which JJ Abrams TV series?

6.
What nickname does Walter White start to go by in *Breaking Bad*?

7.
Which Oscar winner played Sookie Stackhouse in *True Blood*?

8.
When *The Sopranos* finished in 2007, how many seasons had it run for?

9.
Fictional advertising agency Sterling Cooper is the setting for which show?

10.
Which writer and show runner created *The West Wing*?

SO YOU THINK YOU KNOW ...

COUNTRY MUSIC

Quiz 29

1.
Which season of *American Idol* catapulted Carrie Underwood to fame?

2.
"Austin" was the debut single from which artist, who in recent years has been the host of TV show *The Voice*?

3.
What was the name of Taylor Swift's first album, released in 2006?

4.
Which country music star turned pop star cameoed in the 2000 movie *Coyote Ugly*?

5.
After what incident were the Dixie Chicks blacklisted from many radio stations from March 2003?

6.
Which queen of country pop took a break from performing after contracting Lyme disease in 2003?

7.
Which giant of country music died in 2003, just months after his famous wife?

8.
Nicole Kidman wed which country star in 2006?

9.
Dolly Parton was nominated for an Oscar for her song "Travelin' Thru" from which 2005 movie starring Felicity Hoffman?

10.
Who is Tim McGraw married to?

SO YOU THINK
YOU KNOW ...

SMALL SCREEN MEDICS

Quiz 30

1.
Which show is about a stuffy British doctor who relocates to an idyllic seaside town?

2.
Gabriel Byrne stars as a psychotherapist with a slew of revolving clients in which show?

3.
Name the *Grey's Anatomy* character who was spun off to *Private Practice*?

4.
Gregory House from TV show *House MD*, was inspired by which other fictional character?

5.
Doctors Peter Benton, Susan Lewis and Doug Ross were characters on which long-running medical drama?

6.
True or false: fictional hospital Sacred Heart was the setting for TV show *Scrubs*?

7.
Which prolific hit-maker created the plastic surgery-focused show *Nip/Tuck*?

8.
Which actor played a main character in both *Nurse Jackie* and *The Sopranos*?

9.
Which real-life TV plastic surgery show was centered around Dr Robert Rey and his Beverly Hills clients?

10.
Which country singer starred as Dr Clint "Doc" Cassidy in *Doc*, which ran from 2001 to 2004?

SO YOU THINK
YOU KNOW ...

MOVIE
SOUNDTRACKS

"COME GET SOME DINNER.
TINA, EAT. FOOD.
EAT THE FOOD!"

Quiz 31

1.
What song does the cast sing on the bus in 2000's *Almost Famous*?

2.
Who composed the music for the first three Harry Potter movies?

3.
Glen Hansard and Markéta Irglová starred in and sang the soundtrack for which 2007 movie set on the streets of Dublin?

4.
Folk classic "A Man of Constant Sorrow" featured on the soundtrack for which Coen Brothers movie?

5.
Badly Drawn Boy provided the soundtrack to which 2002 Hugh Grant movie?

6.
What four singers sang a cover of "Lady Marmalade" for the *Moulin Rouge!* soundtrack?

7.
What 2002 movie did Eminem win a Best Original Song Oscar for?

8.
Christopher Nolan enlisted Hans Zimmer to write the music for a re-boot of which franchise?

9.
What Jamiroquai song does Napoleon Dynamite dance to at the school assembly?

10.
Name the band and the movie that saw Meryl Streep singing on a Greek Island.

SO YOU THINK
YOU KNOW ...

BEYONCÉ

Quiz 32

1.
What is Beyoncé's full birth name?

2.
Aside from Beyoncé, which other member of Destiny's Child has been there since the start?

3.
What was the name of her first solo album?

4.
In what year was it released?

5.
In what comedy franchise did she make her movie debut?

6.
In 2002, what crime duo did she and Jay-Z sing about?

7.
What was her first solo US number 1 single?

8.
In what year did Destiny's Child officially disband?

9.
What's the name of her alter ego?

10.
Kanye West's interruption of Taylor Swift's MTV Awards acceptance speech was related to which of Beyoncé's singles?

SO YOU THINK
YOU KNOW ...

DOCOS

Quiz 33

1.
Morgan Spurlock made his name documenting a 30-day period when he ate only what food?

2.
Who narrated the English-language version of *March of the Penguins*?

3.
Bowling for Columbine and *Fahrenheit 9/11* are documentaries by which film maker?

4.
Some Kind of Monster is about which rock group?

5.
The subject of a Werner Herzog 2005 documentary, what animal was Timothy Treadwell studying and filming when he was killed by one?

6.
Which docudrama details two men's unbelievable survival after a series of disasters while mountain climbing in the Peruvian Andes?

7.
French man Philippe Petit's journey between which two buildings was retold in *Man on Wire*?

8.
An Inconvenient Truth, centered around former US president hopeful Al Gore, is about what topic?

9.
The Cove looks at dolphin hunting in which country?

10.
Which well-known author lent his voice to 2008's *Food, Inc*?

LIFESTYLE REALITY TV

Quiz 34

1.

What did Trinny Woodall and Susannah Constantine tell you on their makeover show of the same name?

2.

Duane Chapman is better known by what name, after which his TV show is called?

3.

2004 brought Jo Frost to our attention – what was this stern lady's job?

4.

Ted, Kyan, Thom, Carson and Jai were the hosts of which show, which premiered in 2003?

5.

How many kids did Jon and Kate have?

6.

Say Yes to the Dress chronicles the search for the perfect what?

7.

Which was the first of the Real Housewives franchise to air in 2006?

8.

Ashton Kutcher tricked his friends and filmed it in which show?

9.

Which foul-mouthed chef has unleased tirades on restaurant owners since 2007?

10.

The highly dangerous crab-fishing industry is the premise of which long-running show?

SO YOU THINK YOU KNOW ...

HORROR MOVIES

"I WANT TO PLAY A GAME"

Quiz 35

1.
Which horror spoof movie, starring, written and directed by members of the Wayans family, was released in 2000?

2.
2002's *The Ring* is a remake of a horror movie from which country?

3.
What aptly titled movie features Samuel L Jackson battling reptiles at altitude?

4.
What's the name of the orphan in *Orphan*?

5.
What actor's character is sent flying down the street on fire in a wheelchair in 2002's *Red Dragon*?

6.
Cillian Murphy wakes up in what deserted city in 2002's *28 Days Later*?

7.
Strange goings-on caught on a home camera are at the centre of which supernatural horror?

8.
Which actor brought Patrick Bateman from *American Psycho* to life?

9.
Jigsaw is the killer in which franchise?

10.
British tourists come across a murderous psychopath in the Australian Outback in which 2005 movie?

SO YOU THINK
YOU KNOW ...

OPRAH

Quiz 36

1.
In what decade was Oprah born?

2.
How many times in the noughties did Oprah appear in Forbes Celebrity 100 top 10?

3.
The musical adaptation of which 1985 movie starring Oprah ran on Broadway from 2005 to 2008?

4.
In September 2004, Oprah famously gave away what to almost 300 members of her studio audience?

5.
In what year did she form her own TV network?

6.
Oprah was an early champion of which political figure?

7.
Who is Oprah's best friend?

8.
In 2008, Oprah cameoed as herself as an airline passenger in which NYC-based sitcom?

9.
Oprah provided the voice of Gussy the Goose in a 2006 live action remake of which beloved children's classic?

10.
First published in 2000, what is the name of her magazine?

SO YOU THINK
YOU KNOW ...

INDIE
MOVIES

Quiz 37

1.
A life-size rabbit with a creepy skull face features in which 2001 movie?

2.
Who directed Guy Pearce in 2000's *Memento*?

3.
What part of Clementine, Kate Winslet's character in *Eternal Sunshine of the Spotless Mind*, changes color to indicate if she's in the past or the present?

4.
Michelle Yeoh and Chow Yun-fat starred in which independent action movie of 2000?

5.
Who played the two male leads in *Brokeback Mountain*?

6.
Who directed 2003's *Lost in Translation*?

7.
Which actor-director wrote and starred in 2004's *Garden State*?

8.
Elliot Page and Michael Cera are teenagers dealing with unexpected pregnancy in which 2007 movie?

9.
Who plays Paul Giamatti's buddy on a trip around wine country in 2004's *Sideways*?

10.
Push, a 1996 novel by Sapphire, was adapted into which 2009 film?

SO YOU THINK
YOU KNOW ...

POP

GIRLS

Quiz 38

1.
Which 2000s pop sensation's fans were called Little Monsters?

2.
What area of NYC was J.Lo singing about in "Jenny from the Block"?

3.
What band was Fergie a member of, before she struck out solo?

4.
Who became one of the bestselling Latin artists of all time, releasing her first English language album *Laundry Service* in 2001?

5.
From what 2001 album did the Kylie hit "Can't Get You Out of my Head" come from?

6.
Kelly Clarkson won the first season of which reality TV series in 2002?

7.
Alecia Beth Moore is better known by what stage name?

8.
Which burlesque dance troupe turned pop star group who had a hit with "Don't Cha"?

9.
Who sang "Murder on the Dancefloor"?

10.
Britney Spears released a cover of what rock anthem as part of her 2002 movie *Crossroads*?

SO YOU THINK
YOU KNOW ...

SITCOMS

"PIVOT! PIVOT!"

Quiz 39

1.
Friends ended in
which year?

2.
Which *Friends* character
got a spin-off in 2006,
which ran for two seasons?

3.
The goings-on of fictional
TV show *TGS with Tracy
Jordan* is the premise for
which show, created by
Tina Fey?

4.
Who narrated
Arrested Development?

5.
David, Tim, Dawn and
Gareth were the main
characters from which
2001 mockumentary?

6.
Who played the title
character in *The Vicar
of Dibley*?

7.
"Have you met Ted?"
is a reoccurring line from
which sitcom that started
in 2005?

8.
Everybody Hates Chris
was based on the teenage
years of which comedian?

9.
Leslie Knope is the
government employee
with heart in which show
that started in 2009?

10.
Who sings the opening
theme song of *The Big
Bang Theory*?

SO YOU THINK
YOU KNOW ...

SHOES

Quiz 40

1.

Alexander McQueen created extreme platforms named for what animal?

2.

Britney Spears was a brand ambassador for which US shoe company?

3.

What type of dance gave its name to a kind of heeless, round-toed shoe?

4.

Stiletto versions of what footwear made an appearance in the 2000s?

5.

Bulky, oversized trainers became fashionable in what sport?

6.

What was special about Heelys?

7.

Which country did Ugg boots originate from?

8.

What was notable about the Vibram Fivefingers, a shoe released in 2006?

9.

What kind of plastic and rubber beach shoe became increasingly popular?

10.

What polarising brand of shoe, originally intended to be a foam boat shoe, debuted in 2001?

SO YOU THINK YOU KNOW ...

FOOD

AND

DRINK

Quiz 41

1.
Which major soft drink brand launched a lurid blue drink sold as a "Berry Cola Fusion"?

2.
Which restaurant topped the list of The World's 50 Best Restaurants five times in the decade?

3.
A British High Court judge ruled that what brand of chip (crisp) was, in fact, a potato chip?

4.
Magnolia Bakery's cupcakes had a run on their doors after featuring in which TV show?

5.
In 2001, which fast food chain delivered its wares to the International Space Station?

6.
Which chef started a crusade to tackle the nutritional content of British school dinners?

7.
In 2002, then US President George W Bush caused a scare when he fainted after choking on what food item?

8.
What pink cocktail dominated the bar scene in the 2000s?

9.
Towards the end of the decade, making chips (crisps) from what green vegetable became a "healthy" alternative?

10.
Cutting out carbs became popular by which diet?

THE

OFFICE

"I'M NOT SUPERSTITIOUS, BUT I AM A LITTLE STITIOUS"

Quiz 42

1.
Who created the original British show on which the US edition is based?

2.
In which year did the US version of *The Office* premiere?

3.
What's the fictional name of the company it's based on?

4.
What's the name of the long-suffering HR employee who Michael can't stand?

5.
What's Dwight's homestead called?

6.
In the season 2 Christmas episode into what does Jim put a note revealing his true feelings for Pam?

7.
Where do Pam and Jim get officially married?

8.
What's the name of the awards Michael gives out to his employees?

9.
What's the name of Angela's cat that Dwight kills?

10.
Which member of the cast uses his real name?

SO YOU THINK
YOU KNOW ...

POP

BOYS

Quiz 43

1.
In 2004, which member of Westlife parted ways with the band?

2.
Justin Timberlake launched his solo career with which album in 2002?

3.
Which two members of chart-topping Backstreet Boys were cousins?

4.
What are the names of the three Jonas Brothers?

5.
Which son of Spanish pop royalty forged his own pop career in 2001, starting with "Hero"?

6.
The music video for which singer's song sees him strip his clothes, skin, muscles and organs from his body, leaving only a dancing skeleton?

7.
Simon, Duncan, Lee and Antony made up which British pop band?

8.
Celebrity was the final studio album from which supergroup?

9.
Who had a 2007 hit with "Grace Kelly"?

10.
Who beat Gareth Gates to win 2002's UK *Pop Idol*?

SO YOU THINK YOU KNOW ...

CELEBRITY SCANDALS

Quiz 44

1.
Who was arrested for throwing a telephone at a New York hotel clerk in 2005?

2.
Who was convicted of grand theft and vandalism after being arrested in a Saks Fifth Avenue store?

3.
What movie was Christian Bale filming when he unleashed a tirade upon a crew member?

4.
In 2004, which American TV personality went to prison for involvement in a financial scandal?

5.
What record producer was convicted in 2009 of the murder of Lana Clarkson?

6.
Justin Timberlake and Janet Jackson had a wardrobe malfunction while performing at which US sporting event?

7.
How many days of her 45-day sentence did Paris Hilton serve in jail?

8.
On the set of which 2005 movie did Brad Pitt and Angelina Jolie meet?

9.
Who infamously jumped on Oprah's couch in 2005, and for whom was he expressing his love?

10.
Who shaved her head while being photographed by paparazzi in 2007?

SO YOU THINK
YOU KNOW ...

VIDEO
GAMES

Quiz 45

1.
What musical instrument–based video game was released in 2005?

2.
Which motion-sensing video game console was launched in 2006?

3.
A diamond over the head of a character in *The Sims* can tell us what?

4.
The *Halo* series was launched in 2001 by which tech giant?

5.
Gran Turismo 3: A-Spec was the first of the series to be released for which console?

6.
What 2004 online multi-player game took place in the world of Azeroth?

7.
What's the name of the protagonist in *Grand Theft Auto: San Andreas*?

8.
What *Legend of Zelda* game was released in 2000?

9.
Online role-playing game *Poptropica*, aimed at younger kids, was created by which author?

10.
A village of anthropomorphic animals is the setting for which 2001 simulation game?

Answers

Quiz 01: 1. 2002 2. Global financial crisis 3. Four 4. It was demoted to a dwarf planet 5. The Netherlands 6. Joseph Ratzinger (Pope Benedict XVI) 7. July 7 2005 8. Concorde 9. December 26 10. 25th Modern Olympic Games

Quiz 02: 1. *Taken* 2. Lara Croft 3. *Die Another Day* and *Quantum of Solace* 4. Guy Ritchie 5. *The Hurt Locker* 6. *The Fast and the Furious* 7. Catwoman 8. Jason Bourne 9. Precogs 10. Joaquin Phoenix

Quiz 03: 1. *Catching Fire* and *Mockingjay* 2. 2007 3. *Artemis Fowl* 4. *Inkheart* 5. The pigeon 6. *His Dark Materials* 7. *Diary of a Wimpy Kid* 8. Quentin Blake 9. The Gruffalo's 10. The Twilight saga

Quiz 04: 1. *Friday Night Lights* 2. *Gilmore Girls* 3. Chino 4. Three 5. Bristol, England 6. *Dawson's Creek* 7. Kristen Bell 8. *Beverly Hills 90210* (*90210* was the re-boot) 9. *Veronica Mars* 10. *One Tree Hill*

Quiz 05: 1. *Chicago* 2. She wore a swan-shaped dress and left multiple ostrich eggs on the red carpet 3. General Maximus Decimus Meridius (*Gladiator*) 4. False, it was won by *Crash* 5. Virginia Woolf 6. *The Departed* 7. *Monster's Ball* 8. *Who Wants to Be a Millionaire?* 9. Heath Ledger 10. *The Curious Case of Benjamin Button*

Quiz 06: 1. Ron Burgundy from *Anchorman* 2. *Miss Congeniality* 3. Kazakhstan 4. *Legally Blonde* 5. Blue Steel 6. *Little Miss Sunshine* 7. *The Simpsons* 8. A jaguar shark 9. Lindsay Lohan and Jamie Lee Curtis 10. *Snatch*

Quiz 07: 1. Justin Bieber 2. Trucker hats 3. Ed Hardy 4. Baby blue 5. Burberry 6. Metrosexual 7. Mike Tyson 8. Sacha Baron Cohen, dressed as Borat 9. A copy of Jennifer Lopez's Grammy Awards chiffon and silk green dress 10. P. Diddy

Quiz 08: 1. Five 2. Cathy Freeman 3. Rugby union 4. Tiger Woods 5. Paula Radcliffe 6. Washington Wizards 7. Thirteen 8. Usain Bolt's bolt 9. 2007 10. Michael Phelps

Quiz 09: 1. *RuPaul's Drag Race* 2. *The Apprentice* 3. *Britain's Got Talent* 4. Borneo 5. Tyra Banks, *America's Next Top Model* 6. Weight 7. *The X Factor* 8. US$1 million 9. *I'm a Celebrity ... Get Me Out of Here!* 10. *Joe Millionaire*

Quiz 10: 1. 50 Cent 2. Dido, "Thank you" 3. Pharrell Williams 4. Chamillionaire 5. Erykah Badu 6. "Gravel Pit" 7. Missy Elliott 8. Kid Cudi 9. A dance move 10. "Gangsta Lovin'"

Quiz 11: 1. Harvard University 2. Blog early, blog often 3. 140 4. Tom (Thomas Anderson, a Myspace founder) 5. Ronaldinho 6. LinkedIn 7. Photos 8. 2006 9. Tumblr 10. OkCupid

Quiz 12: 1. Kryptonite 2. Amy Lee 3. Linkin Park 4. Sheffield 5. Benji and Joel Madden 6. Green Day (*American Idiot*) 7. Yeah Yeah Yeahs 8. Nirvana 9. The Killers 10. Damon Albarn

Quiz 13: 1. McLovin 2. Their skin sparkles 3. Cheerleading 4. *The Princess Diaries* 5. *Loser* 6. Four 7. Drew Barrymore 8. The "Thriller" dance 9. *Adventureland* 10. Matthew Perry

Quiz 14: 1. Versace 2. Juicy Couture 3. Rachel Zoe 4. Love. Angel. Music. Baby. 5. A hair style where the hair is pulled tightly back off the face and held in a bun or ponytail 6. A Birkin handbag 7. Stella McCartney 8. Boho-chic 9. In a zigzag pattern 10. Madonna, *Music*

Quiz 15: 1. 2009 2. James Cameron 3. *Gone With the Wind* and *Titanic* 4. The Lord of the Rings 5. Sam Worthington 6. Pandora 7. Na'vi 8. Unobtainium 9. He's been promised they will fix his paralysed legs 10. James Horner

Quiz 16: 1. Nicole Richie and Paris Hilton 2. *The Bachelorette* 3. *Laguna Beach* 4. *The Hills* 5. 2007 6. The Playboy mansion 7. *Jersey Shore* 8. *Kourtney and Kim Take Miami* 9. Nick Lachey and Jessica Simpson 10. Kelly Osbourne

Quiz 17: 1. Bratz 2. Razor scooter 3. Sillybandz 4. Lego 5. Who Wants to be a Millionaire 6. iDog 7. 2001 8. Mary-Kate and Ashley Olsen 9. Yu-Gi-Oh! 10. Ticket to Ride

Quiz 18: 1. Florida 2. Benazir Bhutto 3. Ken Livingstone 4. German Chancellor 5. Australia 6. Carla Bruni 7. The United Nations 8. Gibraltar 9. 2009 10. Gordon Brown

Quiz 19: 1. Six 2. It's made of tentacles 3. Beowulf 4. Amy Adams 5. *Night at the Museum* 6. *Underworld* 7. The Scorpion King 8. Wellington, New Zealand 9. Spain 10. The White Witch Jadis

Quiz 20: 1. Downloading music 2. Napster 3. Kindle 4. 2001 5. 4, 8 and 16 GBs 6. An Android operating system 7. Blu-ray Disc 8. Fitbit Tracker 9. Microsoft 10. Wikipedia

Quiz 21: 1. Robert Langdon 2. *Wolf Hall* 3. *Cloud Atlas* 4. *Oryx and Crake* 5. *American Gods* 6. Zadie Smith 7. *The Curious Incident of the Dog in the Night-Time* by Mark Haddon 8. Italy, India and Indonesia 9. Stieg Larsson 10. *The Lovely Bones*

Quiz 22: 1. Africa 2. The Plastics 3. "Jingle Bell Rock" 4. A bath and body store 5. *Queen Bees and Wannabes* by Rosalind Wiseman 6. Tina Fey 7. Nutrition bars 8. The Burn Book 9. Drug dealing 10. She's hit by a school bus

Quiz 23: 1. *Catch Me If You Can* 2. Joel and Ethan Coen 3. John F Kennedy Airport in New York 4. *Band of Brothers* 5. True 6. Paul Newman 7. *My Big Fat Greek Wedding* 8. *The Da Vinci Code* and *Angels and Demons* 9. Wilson 10. Julia Roberts

Quiz 24: 1. Dolly the sheep 2. Go into space 3. The Human Genome Project 4. Seven 5. Ireland 6. HIV 7. Full face transplant 8. SARS (Severe acute respiratory syndrome) 9. 2006 10. 2003

Quiz 25: 1. Chris Farley 2. Tia Carrere 3. Ice Age 4. *Monsters Inc* 5. *Spirited Away* 6. Patton Oswalt 7. Neil Gaiman 8. *Fantastic Mr. Fox* 9. *Up* 10. Dory

Quiz 26: 1. Brad Pitt and Jennifer Aniston 2. Nicole Kidman 3. *Gigli* 4. Rachel McAdams and Ryan Gosling 5. St. Andrews University in Scotland 6. Ryan Reynolds 7. Kevin Federline 8. Mel B (Brown) 9. Mila Kunis 10. Michelle Williams and Heath Ledger

Quiz 27: 1. *Into the Wild* 2. The death of Diana, Princess of Wales 3. Gus Van Sant 4. Frida Kahlo 5. *The Diving Bell and the Butterfly* 6. Steve Coogan 7. *Erin Brockovich* 8. *In Cold Blood* 9. *Hunger* 10. Cate Blanchett

Quiz 28: 1. *The Wire* 2. Mary-Louise Parker 3. Forensic technician for the police 4. Airplane crash 5. *Alias* 6. Heisenberg 7. Anna Paquin 8. Six 9. *Mad Men* 10. Aaron Sorkin

Quiz 29: 1. Season 4 2. Blake Shelton 3. Taylor Swift 4. LeAnn Rimes 5. They criticized President George W Bush 6. Shania Twain 7. Johnny Cash 8. Keith Urban 9. *Transamerica* 10. Faith Hill

Quiz 30: 1. *Doc Martin* 2. *In Treatment* 3. Addison Montgomery 4. Sherlock Holmes 5. *ER* 6. True 7. Ryan Murphy 8. Edie Falco 9. *Dr 90210* 10. Billy Ray Cyrus

Quiz 31: 1. "Tiny Dancer", Elton John 2. John Williams 3. *Once* 4. *O Brother, Where Art Thou?* 5. *About a Boy* 6. Pink, Lil' Kim, Christina Aguilera and Mýa 7. *8 Mile* 8. Batman 9. "Canned Heat" 10. ABBA, *Mamma Mia!*

Quiz 32: 1. Beyoncé Giselle Knowles 2. Kelly Rowland 3. *Dangerously in Love* 4. 2003 5. Austin Powers 6. Bonnie and Clyde 7. "Crazy in Love" 8. 2006 9. Sasha Fierce 10. "Single Ladies (Put a ring on it)"

Quiz 33: 1. McDonald's 2. Morgan Freeman 3. Michael Moore 4. Metallica 5. Bears 6. *Touching the Void* 7. The World Trade Towers, New York 8. Climate change 9. Japan 10. Michael Pollan

Quiz 34: 1. What not to wear 2. *Dog The Bounty Hunter* 3. Nanny 4. *Queer Eye for the Straight Guy* 5. Eight 6. Wedding dress 7. *The Real Housewives of Orange County* 8. *Punk'd* 9. Gordon Ramsay 10. *Deadliest Catch*

Quiz 35: 1. *Scary Movie* 2. Japan (*Ring*) 3. *Snakes on a Plane* 4. Esther 5. Philip Seymour Hoffman 6. London 7. *Paranormal Activity* 8. Christian Bale 9. Saw 10. *Wolf Creek*

Quiz 36: 1. 1950s (1954) 2. Ten 3. *The Color Purple* 4. Cars 5. 2008 6. Barack Obama 7. Gayle King 8. *30 Rock* 9. *Charlotte's Web* 10. O

Quiz 37: 1. *Donnie Darko* 2. Christopher Nolan 3. Her hair 4. *Crouching Tiger, Hidden Dragon* 5. Heath Ledger and Jake Gyllenhaal 6. Sofia Coppola 7. Zach Braff 8. *Juno* 9. Thomas Haden Church 10. *Precious*

Quiz 38: 1. Lady Gaga 2. The Bronx 3. Black Eyed Peas 4. Shakira 5. *Fever* 6. *American Idol* 7. Pink 8. The Pussycat Dolls 9. Sophie Ellis Bextor 10. "I Love Rock 'n' Roll", by Joan Jett & the Blackhearts

Quiz 39: 1. 2004 2. Joey 3. *30 Rock* 4. Ron Howard 5. *The Office* 6. Dawn French 7. *How I Met Your Mother* 8. Chris Rock 9. *Parks and Recreation* 10. Barenaked Ladies

Quiz 40: 1. Armadillo 2. Skechers 3. Ballet (ballet flats) 4. Sneakers 5. Skateboarding 6. They had a wheel in the sole 7. Australia 8. They contoured around the feet, including around the toes. 9. Thongs/flip-flops 10. Crocs

Quiz 41: 1. Pepsi 2. El Bulli 3. Pringles 4. *Sex and the City* 5. Pizza Hut 6. Jamie Oliver 7. A pretzel 8. The Cosmopolitan 9. Kale 10. Atkins

Quiz 42: 1. Ricky Gervais and Stephen Merchant 2. 2005 3. Dunder Mifflin Paper Company 4. Toby 5. Schrute Farms 6. A teapot 7. On a boat below Niagara Falls 8. The Dundees 9. Sprinkles 10. Creed Bratton

Quiz 43: 1. Brian McFadden 2. *Justified* 3. Brian and Kevin 4. Kevin, Joe and Nick 5. Enrique Iglesias 6. Robbie Williams, "Rock DJ" 7. Blue 8. NSYNC 9. Mika 10. Will Young

Quiz 44: 1. Russell Crowe 2. Winona Ryder 3. *Terminator Salvation* 4. Martha Stewart 5. Phil Spector 6. 2004 Super Bowl 7. Three 8. *Mr & Mrs Smith* 9. Tom Cruise, Katie Holmes 10. Britney Spears

Quiz 45: 1. *Guitar Hero* 2. Nintendo Wii 3. The mood of the character 4. Microsoft 5. PlayStation 2 6. *World of Warcraft* 7. Carl "CJ" Johnson 8. *Majora's Mask* 9. Jeff Kinney, author of the Diary of a Wimpy Kid series 10. *Animal Crossing*

Published in 2023 by Smith Street Books
Naarm (Melbourne) | Australia
smithstreetbooks.com

ISBN: 978-1-9227-5485-1

Smith Street Books respectfully acknowledges the Wurundjeri
People of the Kulin Nation, who are the Traditional Owners of the
land on which we work, and we pay our respects to their Elders
past and present.

The moral right of the author has been asserted.

Publisher: Paul McNally
Text: Aisling Coughlan
Editor: Sophie Dougall
Designer: Vanessa Masci
Layout: Heather Menzies, Studio 31
Project manager: Aisling Coughlan
Cover illustration: Paul Borchers
Proofreader: Pamela Dunne

Printed & bound in China by C&C Offset Printing Co., Ltd.

Book 289
10 9 8 7 6 5 4 3 2 1